50 Best

Salsas

&

Dips

50 Best
Salsas
&
Dips

Jane Kirby

A John Boswell Associates/King Hill Productions Book

Broadway Books/New York

BROADWAY

50 BEST SALSAS AND DIPS.
Copyright © 1998 John Boswell Management, Inc., and King Hill Productions.
All rights reserved. Printed in the United States of America. No part of this
book may be reproduced or transmitted in any form or by any means,
electronic or mechanical, including photocopying, recording, or by any
information storage and retrieval system, without written permission from
the publisher. For information, address Broadway Books, a division of
Bantam Doubleday Dell Publishing Group, Inc.,
1540 Broadway, New York, NY 10036.

Broadway Books titles may be purchased for business or
promotional use or for special sales. For information, please write to:
Special Markets Department, Bantam Doubleday Dell Publishing Group, Inc.,
1540 Broadway, New York, NY 10036.

BROADWAY BOOKS and its logo, a letter B bisected on the
diagonal, are trademarks of Broadway Books, a division of
Bantam Doubleday Dell Publishing Group, Inc.

Library of Congress Cataloging-in-Publication Data

Kirby, Jane, 1953–
    50 best salsas & dips / Jane Kirby
        p. cm. — ("A John Boswell Associates/King Hill Productions book.")
    Includes index.
    ISBN 0-7679-0081-2 (pbk.)
    1. Salsas (Cookery) 2. Dips (Appetizers) I. Title. II. Series.
    TX819.S29K57 1998
    641.8′14—dc21   97-52703
                                                          CIP

FIRST EDITION

Illustration and design by Richard Oriolo

98 99 00 01 02   10 9 8 7 6 5 4 3 2 1

Contents

Introduction / 1

Salsas: Some Hot, Some Not / 7

Almost Instant Dips / 21

Garlicky and Great / 31

Best of the Beans / 43

Especially Hot and Sassy / 53

Artfully Elegant / 67

Cheddar and Better / 79

Chips, Crisps, and Other Dippers / 87

Index / 93

To Austin, Morgan, Grant, Eliza, and Jacob,

who allowed me to dip into their lives.

50 Best

Salsas

&

Dips

Introduction

The Life of the Party

When it comes to party pleasers, salsas or dips are always popular—and with good reason. Nothing is easier for the cook than to throw a few ingredients into the food processor, whirl them together for a few seconds, and scoop the resulting blend into a serving bowl. A basket of chips or an assortment of cut-up raw vegetables, and voilà—it's a party! And everything can be prepared in advance.

As a professional food editor as well as an accomplished cook, I've been asked many times to help cater friends' cocktail parties or to organize the food for a function at my son's school. My suggestion is always the same. Do a collection of dips and salsas for chips and vegetables, spreads for toasts and crackers. There are several reasons for this advice. They're easy, they can be casual or dressy but they're never fussy, and when folks serve themselves, as they do with this kind of food, it automatically puts them at ease. Over the years I've collected many of these simple but stylish recipes. They're always the life of the party, and they formed the inspiration for this book.

America's appetite for dips is as patriotic as its love of potato chips but much more recent. Potato chips are almost 150 years old, but dips are a young 40-something. It wasn't until 1954 that Lipton's dry onion soup was blended with sour cream to create the ultimate instant party pleasure: "California Dip." The recipe became a culinary icon that launched an entertaining trend and inspired a generation of cooks. I still love it scooped up with ripple-cut potato chips. (You won't find a recipe for it here, though, because in my opinion, there's no improving on the version on the soup box.)

If we've come a long way in the kitchen since then, it is in large part because of the availability of so many more ingredients. Items such as fresh ginger, arugula, sun-dried tomatoes, farmstead goat cheese, and Mediterranean olives, which were once considered foreign and exotic, are almost as much a part of the pantry now as packaged soup mixes were in the '50s. Extra-virgin olive oil has overtaken mayonnaise, salsa outsells ketchup, and fresh herbs are almost as prevalent as dried.

When it comes to pleasing the palate, it's all about flavor, always has been. In the past we relied on fat to do the job; now we utilize seasonings and often aim for a taste explosion of spicy ingredients. In fact, Americans have developed a passion for fiery foods. A restaurateur friend tells me that when he marks his extra-hot menu items with a skull and crossbones, the dishes fly out of the kitchen. That's why I devoted an entire chapter to recipes that are especially hot and spicy.

Of course, everyone has a favorite flavor, which is why certain other ingredients rated separate chapters, too. Garlic, the food lover's favorite; versatile, fat-free beans; and cheeses of all kinds each have their own. There's also an entire section of "almost-instant" recipes, which can be whipped up in minutes, and a chapter of more elegant ideas for dressier occasions. In the salsa chapter, you'll find red ones and green ones, salsas made with vegetables, and others blended from fruits to give you an idea of the amazing versatility these chunky dipping sauces really possess.

Since what you dip with is important too, I've included a few recipes just in case you feel like making your own chips, toasts, and crisps. Remember, with home baked, you can adjust the flavor and minimize or eliminate the fat.

Make Them a Meal

Maybe it's because I'm a registered dietitian, but I'm a big fan of eating six small meals instead of three squares. I think smaller amounts eaten more often is a healthier way to go. The salsas, dips, and spreads in this book can make delicious, healthful mini-meals or snacks. My nutrition credentials also make me particularly fond of skinny dips, such as salsas, because they're virtually fat free. For example, dollop one of the salsas onto a baked potato and call it lunch. Here are a few more calorie-stretching, flavor-packed ideas:

- Use one of the bean dips for a sandwich filling.
- Replace plain mayonnaise on sandwiches with a lower-fat, more flavorful spread, such as Black Olive and Dried Tomato Tapenade (page 41).
- Heap a fruity salsa onto a broiled chicken breast.
- Dress baked fish fillets with a pungent garlicky spread.
- Extend cheese calories by blending the cheese into spreads and smearing them onto vegetables, rather than by cutting the cheese into wedges and serving with crackers.

Party Planning

No host or hostess wants to slave in the kitchen when there's fun to be had at the party, so whenever possible I've included instructions for making the recipes ahead of time and guidelines for how long they'll stay fresh. (If drop-in guests catch you at the last minute, though, don't forget the "Almost Instant" chapter.)

Though a party of dips, spreads, and salsas means finger foods, have a stack of plates and napkins nearby. That way guests can take away a collection of appetizers to enjoy leisurely without feeling they have to hover over a serving dish. Certainly for most informal gatherings, one wonderful dip is all you'll need. But for larger groups, it's nice to offer an assortment. Three kinds make a good selection. Include a familiar one, a spicy one, and something slightly more unusual. Try for a variety of colors and vary the textures.

When estimating how much you'll need, a good rule of thumb is to plan about ½ cup of dip per guest. And although the recipes here are called dips and salsas, they don't have to be served that way. For example, a dressy cocktail party might include a sliced grilled pork tenderloin sandwiched between corn bread and served with a fruity or spicy salsa. Or perhaps a sliced cold fillet of beef served on French bread with a mayonnaise-based dip and garnished with a sliver or two of sweet pickle.

Serve Them with Style

Don't let the casualness of most of these recipes fool you. Easy appetizers can be presented with style. Be creative. A hollowed-out red cabbage may be a cocktail-party cliché, but a little dip or salsa served in a colorful bell pepper, in a miniature pumpkin, or in a hollowed-out crusty round loaf of bread is still a fresh idea. Place one or two of them strategically around the room to help the traffic flow and alleviate congestion at the main table.

When it comes to displays of food, bigger is almost always better. An oversize basket piled with raw vegetables makes a more dramatic appearance than several bowls. I've done arrangements on wooden cutting boards as well. I'll pull down the antique bowls that hang on my kitchen wall and press them into service. And I'll even admit from time to time to dusting off the old sombrero bowl from the top shelf for tortilla chips and guacamole. The familiar can be fabulous. Here are a few more ideas:

- For springtime parties, pile chips into a (clean, never used) flower pot with a smaller one lined with plastic wrap for the dip or salsa—plug the hole with a radish.
- For a summer pool party, children's sand pails make great containers for vegetables. Sand-castle molds can be used to shape a spread. Use toy dump trucks for chips.
- Large clam shells make good dip servers.

- For a wintry chilled dip, make an ice bowl: Freeze an inch or two of water in a large mixing bowl. Then center a smaller bowl in the larger one and continue to add water to the large bowl a few inches at a time to form a shell of ice. Use a brick or large can to keep the smaller bowl weighted down in place. Ice bowls can be dressed up by adding cranberries or pine sprigs or other nontoxic seasonal greens to the water as it freezes for decoration. When frozen, fill the smaller bowl with hot water and quickly remove it. Then dip the large bowl quickly into hot water and remove it to unmold the ice bowl. Store your ice bowl in the freezer until ready to use.
- Search hardware stores to find unusual holders for dips or dippers: Mason jars, small galvanized metal buckets, wooden nail boxes, and paper paint buckets are all possibilities as containers for bread sticks, chips, and crisps.

So the next time you're looking for inspiration for a cocktail party appetizer, between-meal snack, simple starter, or even a light meal, open this book. Pick one or two recipes, or sample several. There are over 50 nifty sassy salsas and delightful dips to choose from.

Salsas:
Some Hot, Some Not

Today salsa is to tortilla chips what California sour cream and onion dip once was to potato chips. Both pairings are perfect and provide for almost unrestrained nibbling. Both serve the harried host or hostess well in terms of convenience and guaranteed popularity. The differences between a salsa and a rich sour cream- or mayonnaise-based dip, though, are worth noting, because they say a lot about contemporary food fashion.

Unlike the older dips, salsas are usually fat free. They are a combination of finely chopped fruits and vegetables, usually a little chopped onion, all enlivened with a bit of chile and fresh lime juice or vinegar. In fact, the pleasing burst of flavor you experience when you taste a salsa comes partly from that contrast between sweet and spicy. It is the unexpectedness of the taste as well as the mouth-filling complexity of flavor that gives salsa much of its potency and popularity.

Today, salsa can be found in every supermarket in every state. It's old news that its sales have outstripped those of ketchup. But what's new is the variety of flavors and colors in which salsas now appear. As with everything else, though, there is still no substitute for homemade.

Freshly made salsa delivers the kind of flavor punch that can't be contained in a jar, can, or plastic supermarket tub. With the food processor, preparation at home really is by and large quick and easy. Remember also that salsas are not just for dipping. They make great fresh relishes and toppings for all kinds of simply cooked foods, especially chicken, pork, and seafood.

Tip: For a milder onion flavor in any of these recipes, soak the chopped onion in a bowl of very hot tap water for a few minutes. Then dump into a sieve, rinse under cold running water, and shake to drain well.

Fresh Tomato Salsa

Jarred sauce can't hold a flaming jalapeño to freshly made, especially in summer, when sweet, ripe native beefsteak tomatoes are plentiful and cheap. Note that I leave the seeds in the chile peppers here to add a little extra heat. Use this as a base for Chile con Queso (page 86), or serve simply as is with tortilla chips.

4 large ripe tomatoes (about 8 ounces each)
½ medium white onion, chopped
⅓ cup chopped fresh cilantro
1 serrano or 2 jalapeño peppers, minced
3 tablespoons fresh lime juice
¼ teaspoon salt

1. Cut out the tomato cores. Cut the tomatoes crosswise in half and squeeze gently to remove the seeds. Chop the tomatoes.

2. In a medium bowl, combine the chopped tomatoes with the onion, cilantro, serrano or jalapeño peppers, lime juice, and salt. Stir to mix well. Season with additional salt to taste. Serve at room temperature.

Salsa Verde

The English translation of this Mexican condiment, "green sauce," doesn't do it justice. Use this all-purpose dip for tortilla chips, seafood, and burgers and to season tacos and enchiladas—you name it. For a thicker, richer sauce, add a finely chopped avocado.

Tomatillos, which give this sauce its color, look like small green tomatoes with papery outer husks.

¾ pound fresh tomatillos or 1 (11-ounce) can whole tomatillos
2 garlic cloves
2 serrano or 3 jalapeño peppers
2 cups packed fresh cilantro
1 medium white onion, coarsely chopped
¼ teaspoon salt

1. If using fresh tomatillos, peel off the papery outer skins. Bring a large saucepan of water to a boil. Add the tomatillos. As soon as the water returns to a boil, cook for 30 seconds; drain. If using canned, simply drain the tomatillos.

2. Peel the garlic. Cut the stems off the serrano or jalapeño peppers. If you want the salsa milder, cut the peppers in half and remove the seeds. Mince the garlic and peppers by dropping them through the feed tube of a food processor or blender while the machine is turned on.

3. Add the tomatillos, cilantro, onion, and salt to the processor. Process until the tomatillos and onion are chopped. Serve at room temperature.

Cranberry-Orange Salsa

Makes 4 cups

Serve this powerful salsa next Thanksgiving, and you will banish canned cranberry sauce or jelly forever. Sweet spices and a tiny bit of hot pepper add a lovely counterpoint to the tart cranberries, which are softened with just a little sugar and a couple of oranges. At times when fresh cranberries are not available, look for them in the freezer case. Process them without waiting for the berries to thaw; they will defrost by the time the salsa is done. Seed the jalapeño pepper only if you wish to reduce the heat of this salsa.

2 navel oranges
1 small white onion, quartered
2 cups fresh or frozen cranberries
1 jalapeño pepper, minced
2 tablespoons sugar
½ teaspoon ground cumin
¼ teaspoon ground cinnamon
¼ teaspoon salt

1. Scrub the oranges with a kitchen brush and warm soapy water; rinse well and pat dry. Cut each orange into 8 wedges.

2. In a food processor, coarsely chop the oranges and onion by pulsing. Add the cranberries and pulse until all 3 ingredients are finely chopped.

3. Transfer to a bowl and add the jalapeño pepper, sugar, cumin, cinnamon, and salt. Stir to mix well. Set aside at room temperature for about 30 minutes to allow the flavors to blend.

Grilled Corn Salsa with Tomatillos, Peppers, and Lime

Makes 2 cups

This salsa tastes like summer itself. It's particularly good with crab cakes, steak, or grilled or barbecued chicken. If you don't have access to a grill or it's the wrong season and all that's available are canned corn kernels and tomatillos, you can still make a very good salsa. Here's how: If the corn is fresh, cut the kernels from the cob; if canned, drain well. Toast the corn kernels in a large, dry heavy skillet with 1 tablespoon vegetable oil in place of the mayonnaise over medium heat, stirring, until golden brown, about 8 minutes. Stir in the cumin and cook 30 seconds longer, or until fragrant. Drain and chop the tomatillos and add to the corn. Mix with all the remaining ingredients.

3 or 4 ears of fresh corn (to yield 2 cups kernels)
1 tablespoon mayonnaise
5 fresh tomatillos (about ½ pound)
1 teaspoon whole cumin seeds
½ cup finely diced white onion
½ medium green bell pepper, finely diced
1 garlic clove, minced
1 jalapeño pepper, seeded and chopped
2 tablespoons fresh lime juice
½ teaspoon salt
2 tablespoons chopped fresh cilantro

1. Light a medium-hot fire in a charcoal or gas grill. While it's heating, bring a large pot of water to a boil. Shuck the corn and boil for 2 minutes. Remove the corn with tongs and let dry. Brush with mayonnaise to coat lightly. Grill the corn, turning, until lightly browned all over, 3 to 5 minutes. As soon as the ears are cool enough to handle, cut the corn kernels from the cobs.

2. Remove the papery outer skin of the tomatillos. Drop them in a saucepan of boiling water and cook for 30 seconds. Drain and pat dry. Finely dice the tomatillos.

3. In a small dry skillet, toast the cumin seeds over medium heat, shaking the pan often, until fragrant and slightly darkened, about 2 minutes. Crush in a mortar with a pestle or between 2 sheets of wax paper with a heavy rolling pin.

4. In a medium bowl, combine the grilled corn, tomatillos, and toasted cumin with all the remaining ingredients. Stir to mix well. Serve the salsa at room temperature.

Pineapple-Mango Salsa

This salsa has shown up on tony restaurant menus from coast to coast and for good reason: The balance of sweet and spicy, crunchy and tender, salty and tangy explodes in your mouth. Serve it with tortilla chips or on anything from the grill, especially swordfish, shrimp, and chicken.

1 mango
¼ fresh pineapple, finely diced (about 1 ½ cups)
½ cup finely chopped white onion
3 tablespoons chopped fresh mint
2 tablespoons fresh lime juice
¼ teaspoon cayenne
⅛ teaspoon salt

1. Peel the mango by slipping a small knife under the skin at one end and peeling back a wide strip of skin. Repeat all around the mango. Cut as much fruit as possible off the large flat pit in the center. (Or use the technique described on page 15.) Finely dice the mango.

2. In a medium bowl, combine the mango, pineapple, and onion. Toss lightly to mix.

3. Add the mint, lime juice, cayenne, and salt. Stir and fold to mix. Taste and season with additional cayenne and salt to taste. Serve slightly chilled or at room temperature.

How to Peel a Mango

If you've been stumped by a mango because you couldn't cut the fruit from its skin or from the tenacious large, flat pit without mangling it, try this technique: Hold the whole fruit on end and use a large, sharp knife to slice as much fruit as possible in one piece from each of the long, flat sides, cutting as close to the pit as you can. Using a small knife, score the flesh in a diamond pattern up to, but not through, the skin. Turn the scored mango halves inside out by pushing from the skin side with your thumbs. Then cut the cubed fruit from the skin; it will come off easily.

Minted Peach Salsa with Toasted Pecans

Makes 3 cups

The success of this salsa depends on ripe peaches. Look for rosy fruits with an underlying yellow, rather than greenish, cast. They should smell fragrant and yield to gentle pressure. Off season, you can use an equal amount of frozen peaches (packaged without sugar). Serve this slightly sweet salsa with ham, roast pork, barbecued ribs, or grilled chicken.

1/2 cup pecan pieces or slivered almonds
3 ripe peaches, peeled and finely diced
1 small red bell pepper, seeded and finely diced
1/2 cup chopped red onion
1/2 cup fresh mint leaves, chopped
1 garlic clove, minced
3 tablespoons fresh lime juice

1. Preheat the oven to 325°F. Spread out the nuts in a single layer on a small baking sheet and toast in the oven, stirring 2 or 3 times, until lightly browned, 7 to 10 minutes. Be sure to keep an eye on them, because nuts burn quickly. Transfer to a cutting board and let cool, then coarsely chop.

2. Plunge the peaches into a medium saucepan of boiling water and count to 10. Remove the peaches and cool under cold running water. Coax the peel off with a small knife. Finely dice the peaches.

3. In a medium bowl, combine the toasted pecans and peaches with the bell pepper, red onion, mint, garlic, and lime juice. Stir to mix well. If made ahead, cover and refrigerate for up to 1 day. Serve at room temperature.

Watermelon Salsa

This sweet and lively salsa is delightful served with freshly baked tortilla chips that have been dusted with chili powder and a little sugar or with Wonton Crisps (page 89). It's also good with grilled or baked pork chops. Since watermelon is now available year-round, the refreshing taste of summer is only minutes away.

1 ½ pounds watermelon
¼ cup salted roasted peanuts
¼ cup packed fresh mint
¼ cup packed fresh basil
2 scallions, finely chopped
2 tablespoons fresh lime juice
¼ teaspoon salt

1. Cut the watermelon into ½-inch-thick slices. Cut off and discard the rind. Pick out any seeds and cut the watermelon into ⅜-inch dice. (There will be about 2 cups.)

2. Combine the peanuts, mint, and basil in a food processor. Pulse to chop.

3. Place the watermelon in a medium bowl. Add the chopped peanuts, mint, and basil along with the scallions, lime juice, and salt. Stir to mix well. Serve slightly chilled or at room temperature.

Roasted Vegetable Salsa

Makes 1 ¾ cups

For a richer flavor here, I char the tomatoes, garlic, jalapeño peppers, and onions before blending them with the other ingredients. An outdoor grill, of course, will add the best smoky taste, but a stove-top griddle or a broiler can also be used.

8 large plum tomatoes
1 medium white onion, peeled and sliced
2 jalapeño peppers, cut lengthwise in half
3 garlic cloves, not peeled
⅓ cup chopped fresh basil
1 tablespoon balsamic vinegar
2 teaspoons fresh lemon juice
¼ teaspoon salt
Freshly ground pepper

1. Light a medium-hot fire in a barbecue grill or lightly oil a stove-top griddle or cast-iron skillet and heat until hot. Alternatively, preheat a broiler with the rack set as close to the heat as possible.

2. Grill or broil the tomatoes, onion, jalapeño peppers, and garlic, turning, until the tomatoes and peppers are charred all over and the onion slices and garlic are browned, 4 to 6 minutes.

3. Peel the tomatoes, cut them in half, and squeeze gently to remove the seeds. Peel the jalapeño peppers, stem them, and remove the seeds if you want to reduce the heat. Remove the garlic cloves from their skins. With a large sharp knife, coarsely chop the tomatoes and onion slices. Finely chop the jalapeños and garlic.

4. In a medium bowl, combine all the chopped vegetables. Mix well. Stir in the basil, balsamic vinegar, lemon juice, and salt. Season generously with pepper to taste. Serve at room temperature.

Banana Salsa

Here's a robust fruity salsa to scoop up with plantain or root vegetable chips or to spoon over grilled fish. The vegetables give body to the mélange, and the banana lends an earthy sweetness. This salsa is also good with tortilla chips that have been dusted with ground cinnamon.

1 large banana, peeled and finely diced
1 jalapeño pepper, minced
½ cup finely chopped white onion
1 small red bell pepper, seeded and chopped
3 tablespoons fresh lime juice
2 tablespoons chopped fresh cilantro
1 tablespoon unsulphured molasses
¼ teaspoon salt

Combine all the ingredients in a small bowl. Stir gently to mix. Serve at room temperature.

Orange-Jicama Salsa

Makes about 3 cups

Jicama is a root vegetable with a smooth brown skin. It must be peeled and trimmed of coarse outer fibers before using. Look for it in Latin groceries and in the exotic produce department of your supermarket. Water chestnuts or a mild, tart apple, such as a Granny Smith, would make an acceptable substitute.

2 navel oranges
1 small jicama
6 radishes, finely diced
½ cup finely diced red onion
3 tablespoons fresh lime juice
1 teaspoon chili powder
¼ teaspoon salt
⅓ cup chopped fresh cilantro

1. Cut off all the skin and bitter white pith from the oranges. Working over a bowl to catch the juices, cut down between the membranes to release the segments. Finely dice the oranges. Add to the juice in the bowl.

2. Use a swivel-bladed vegetable peeler or sharp paring knife to remove the brown skin from the jicama. Cut the vegetable into ¼-inch dice; there should be 1½ to 2 cups. Add to the oranges.

3. Add the radishes, red onion, lime juice, chili powder, and salt. If not serving soon, cover and refrigerate for up to 3 hours. Stir in the chopped cilantro just before serving.

Almost Instant
Dips

Here are some easy dips and spreads to turn to when you need an appetizer with dash in a flash. All these recipes are simple to stir together or whirl together in the blender or food processor; all will turn out an excellent dip or spread in five minutes or less. And they're made with ingredients that are most likely already on your shelf or that can be picked up with a quick stop at any local market.

While all are surprisingly fast and easy, you'll find many are special enough to make a fine showing at the dressiest cocktail party. They can rescue an otherwise ordinary dinner or stretch take-out or freezer fare into a menu that is company compatible. All you need add are a basket of tortilla chips, pita triangles, or potato chips, or a platter of colorful raw or lightly cooked vegetables to dunk with, or some good bread or crackers on which to smooth your spread.

For a more substantial starter, many of the dips pair beautifully with an assortment of hot and cold finger foods: cooked shrimp, chicken nuggets or wings, spareribs, or Chinese dumplings, for example. And the flavored mayonnaises, whether curried or fired up with chipotle chiles, can form the base of a most interesting tuna, chicken, or shellfish salad.

As is typical of classic dips, a majority of these start with jarred mayonnaise or sour cream. If you find the calories or fat threatening, reduced- or low-fat products can be substituted. If you use these lighter products regularly, the difference in taste will probably seem negligible.

Clam Digger's Dip

Bring out the potato chips and dunk away; you won't be able to stop. This classic is to New England what sour cream and onion dip is to California. I've just updated it a bit by adding some extra heat.

1 cup sour cream
1 tablespoon Worcestershire sauce
¼ teaspoon salt
Pinch of powdered mustard
⅛ teaspoon hot pepper sauce, or more to taste
1 (6½-ounce) can minced clams
Paprika

1. In a small bowl, combine the sour cream with the Worcestershire sauce, salt, powdered mustard, and hot sauce. Stir to blend well.

2. Drain the minced clams, reserving the broth for another use, if you wish. Add the clams to the sour cream base and stir to mix well. Cover with plastic wrap and refrigerate for 30 minutes to allow the flavors to develop. This dip keeps well for at least 2 days.

3. To serve, spoon into a small bowl and dust the top with paprika. Serve chilled.

Tuna and Anchovy Dip

Makes 1¾ cups

Based on the classic Italian *tonnato sauce often used to cloak chilled slices of veal as a summer dinner, this makes a tangy dunk for crudités all year-round. It's lemony and hearty and is best paired with any raw, crunchy vegetable. Cauliflower or broccoli florets, carrot sticks, red pepper strips, and fresh fennel sticks are especially good choices.*

For convenience, 1 tablespoon of anchovy paste can be substituted for the canned flat anchovy fillets, but the resulting taste will be a bit milder.

1 (6½-ounce) can tuna, drained and flaked
½ (2-ounce) can flat anchovies, 3 or 4 fillets
1 cup mayonnaise
¼ cup capers
½ teaspoon paprika
¼ teaspoon salt
2 to 3 tablespoons fresh lemon juice
Freshly ground pepper

1. In a blender or food processor, combine the tuna, anchovies, mayonnaise, capers, paprika, salt, and 2 tablespoons lemon juice. Puree until smooth.

2. Taste and add the remaining lemon juice and pepper to taste. If not using at once, cover and refrigerate until serving time.

Red-Hot Orange Spiced Dip

A lively accompaniment to grilled foods, this Asian-accented dip also works wonders on grilled strips of pork tenderloin, spareribs, or chicken fingers, and it makes an excellent updated alternative to duck sauce for Chinese dumplings. It is astonishingly effective with fried calamari, affording a pleasant change from the usual tartar sauce or heavy marinara. Rice vinegar is available in the Asian section of most supermarkets. Be sure to choose the unseasoned variety for general cooking.

1 cup orange marmalade
¼ cup rice vinegar
1 teaspoon crushed hot pepper flakes
½ teaspoon salt
¼ teaspoon ground cinnamon
¼ teaspoon ground cumin

1. In a small bowl, combine the marmalade, vinegar, hot pepper, salt, cinnamon, and cumin. Stir until well blended.

2. If you have the time, let the dip stand for about 30 minutes to allow the flavors to develop. Season with additional salt to taste just before serving. Any leftover dip will keep well in the refrigerator in a covered jar for up to 2 weeks.

Watercress Dip

This bright green dip makes a dazzling presentation with carrot sticks or chilled cooked shrimp. It's also nice as an alternative to tartar sauce or as a sandwich spread in place of plain mayonnaise. Fresh spinach leaves can be substituted for the watercress. The dip will have the same vivid color, though it will lack the peppery bite watercress imparts.

    1 cup watercress leaves
    ¼ cup flat-leaf parsley sprigs, tough stems removed
    2 scallions, cut into 2-inch pieces
    1 cup mayonnaise
    1 tablespoon fresh lemon juice
    ¼ teaspoon salt
    Freshly ground pepper
    Dash of hot pepper sauce, or more to taste

1. In a food processor, combine the watercress, parsley, and scallions. Pulse, scraping down the bowl once or twice, until chopped.

2. Add the mayonnaise, lemon juice, salt, pepper, and hot sauce. Whirl just until blended to keep flecks of green or process until the herbs are pureed and the entire mixture is pale green, depending upon the look you prefer; the taste will be the same.

3. Season with additional lemon juice, salt, and pepper to taste. If not serving at once, cover and refrigerate for up to 3 hours.

Variations

Arugula Dip—Substitute 1¼ cups arugula for the watercress and parsley. The dip will be pungent and very peppery.

Pesto Dip—Substitute 1 cup fresh basil leaves for the watercress. Reduce the parsley to 2 tablespoons. Add 1 garlic clove crushed through a press and 2 tablespoons freshly grated Parmesan or Romano cheese in Step 2.

Bombay Curry Dip

Makes about 1 1/2 cups

Here's a cocktail party standby that can't be beat. A bowl of vibrant yellow curried mayonnaise placed in the center of a basket, surrounded by a rainbow of colorful cut-up vegetables or mountains of pink cooked shrimp, can form the popular core of any buffet spread. It also makes a spectacular curried chicken salad, with some raisins, slivered almonds, and diced tart apple added to your basic recipe.

If the taste of raw garlic is a little too sharp for your palate, you can mellow the bite by mincing the garlic with the salt until it forms a paste before blending it with the other ingredients. If you have a little extra time, the energy, and the enthusiasm, toast the curry powder in a dry skillet for a minute or two, until the seasoning releases its fragrance. The resulting flavor will be deeper and more mellow.

1 cup mayonnaise
1/4 cup milk
4 teaspoons curry powder
1/3 cup fresh lemon juice
1 small garlic clove, minced
1/2 teaspoon paprika
1/2 teaspoon salt
1/2 teaspoon sugar

Combine all the ingredients in a small bowl. Stir until well blended. Taste and adjust the salt and sugar as needed.

Chipotle Mayonnaise

With its propensity for enlivening corn on the cob, this terra-cotta–colored mayonnaise should be a summer staple. It also serves well as a spread with Southwestern-flavored grilled meats, such as fajitas, on chicken sandwiches, and as a mildly spicy, slightly smoky dip for tortilla chips.

2 ounces chipotle chiles in adobo sauce (about ¼ cup)
1 (6- to 7-ounce) jar roasted red peppers, drained and rinsed
1 cup mayonnaise
1 teaspoon ground cumin
1 teaspoon chopped fresh oregano or ½ teaspoon dried
¼ teaspoon salt

1. In a food processor or blender, combine the chipotle chiles with any sauce that clings to them and the roasted peppers. Puree until smooth. Scrape down the sides of the bowl.

2. Add the mayonnaise, cumin, oregano, and salt. Blend well. Cover and refrigerate until serving time.

Note: For more mellow flavor, toast the cumin in a small skillet over medium-low heat, stirring often, for 2 to 3 minutes, until fragrant before adding.

Chutney Ham Spread

Makes 1½ cups

Nothing is easier than this tangy, slightly sweet spread. As a passed hors d'oeuvre, it's wonderful on mini corn muffins or old-fashioned baking powder biscuits cut with a 1½-inch cutter or spooned into tiny cocktail puffs. Try it spread on small squares of rye or whole-grain bread to make mini sandwiches and pile them high on a napkin-lined serving tray.

½ pound honey-baked ham
3 tablespoons mango chutney
2 tablespoons unsalted butter, softened
1 tablespoon Cognac or brandy (optional)
1½ teaspoons powdered mustard
⅛ teaspoon hot pepper sauce

1. Trim any excess fat from the ham and cut the meat into 1-inch dice. Place the ham in a food processor and pulse until chopped.

2. Add the chutney, butter, Cognac, mustard, and hot sauce. Pulse briefly to mix. Serve slightly chilled or at room temperature.

30   5 0   B e s t   S a l s a s   a n d   D i p s

Garlicky
and Great

Who would ever guess that garlic would become one of America's favorite flavors. For those who love the alluring allium, it's hard to get too much of a good thing. The dips and spreads in this chapter have a distinctly Mediterranean cast—not a surprise given garlic's prominent place in southern Italian, provincial French, Greek, and Lebanese cooking.

When garlic is to be used raw, freshness is paramount. Underneath the outer skins, look for firm, white cloves that are moist when cut, with no trace of green shoots. If it's one of those in-between seasons and all the garlic around seems to be sprouting, pry out the thin green center with the tip of a small knife before mincing or crushing the cloves. This is especially important if the garlic is to be used raw. If cooked, the difference probably won't be noticeable.

Baba Ganoush

Makes about 3 ½ cups

If you've been eating more vegetarian meals lately, as I have, you'll find this versatile Middle Eastern dip a wonderful additional to your repertoire. Baba ganoush's tart, garlicky, slightly nutty taste also makes it a satisfying addition to almost any plate of vegetables or salads. It's perfect as an easy but interesting spread for a party, too. Just pass a basket of toasted pita wedges on the side. For extra smoky flavor, be sure to char the eggplant thoroughly.

> 2 medium eggplants (1 pound each)
> ⅓ cup tahini (Middle Eastern sesame paste)
> ⅓ cup fresh lemon juice
> 3 garlic cloves, crushed through a press
> 1 teaspoon salt
> 2 tablespoons chopped parsley

1. Light a hot fire in a barbecue grill or preheat the broiler with the rack set about 6 inches from the heat. Puncture the eggplants with the tip of a small knife in a couple of spots and grill or broil, turning, until they are charred outside and completely soft inside, 15 to 20 minutes. Remove and let cool.

2. When they can be handled, cut the eggplants in half and with a large spoon, scoop the flesh off the blackened skin into a bowl. Add the tahini to the warm eggplant and stir and mash until the sesame paste is completely blended in and the eggplant is smooth and slightly creamy.

32   **5 0   B e s t   S a l s a s   a n d   D i p s**

3. Beat in the lemon juice, garlic, and salt. Turn into a serving dish and garnish with the chopped parsley. This dip keeps well, covered, in the refrigerator for up to 5 days.

Note: Tahini, Middle Eastern sesame paste, comes in a can. The oil and paste are often separated, so be sure to mix them together before using. Store in the refrigerator after opening.

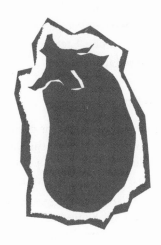

Roasted Garlic Spread

Makes about 1 cup

Roasting mellows and sweetens garlic without taking away any of its fabulously enticing taste. Spread this over crostini, on roast beef sandwiches, or over grilled vegetables. Artichokes dipped into this spread are sublime. Lightly cooked asparagus spears or triangles of multi-colored sweet peppers, which are spectacular looking arranged on a platter, are also good dunkers.

> 4 heads of garlic
> 1/3 cup chicken broth
> 2 tablespoons dry white wine
> 4 large sprigs of fresh thyme plus 1 teaspoon fresh thyme leaves or
> > 1 1/4 teaspoons dried thyme leaves
> 1/4 cup extra-virgin olive oil
> 1 tablespoon fresh lemon juice
> 1/4 teaspoon salt

1. Preheat the oven to 425°F. Remove the dry, papery outer skins from each whole head of garlic but do not separate the cloves. Cut off and discard the top of each head to expose the tops of the cloves inside.

2. Arrange the garlic heads upright in a single layer in a small baking dish or pie plate. Pour the chicken broth and wine over them and lay the thyme sprigs on top of the garlic. (If using dried thyme, sprinkle 1 teaspoon over the heads of garlic.) Cover the dish with aluminum foil and bake until the garlic is very soft and golden but not brown, 45 to 60 minutes. Remove from the oven and let cool, reserving any liquid that remains in the baking dish.

3. Slip the garlic from their skins by squeezing the cloves between your fingers. Place the peeled roasted garlic in a blender or food processor. Add the reserved baking liquid (if there is any), the olive oil, lemon juice, fresh thyme leaves or ¼ teaspoon dried, and the salt. Puree until smooth. If made ahead, transfer to a small bowl, cover, and refrigerate for up to 3 days. Serve the spread at room temperature.

Creamy Garlic and Anchovy Dip

Makes about 2 cups

The Italians call this bagna cauda, *and they serve it with fresh vegetables or bread sticks. It also makes an unusual dip for fried clams or steamed shrimp. This recipe calls for a stunning amount of garlic—three heads or about 54 cloves, but don't be put off. After simmering in milk for over half an hour, it mellows to an irresistible sweetness. While you'll end up with about 2 cups of dip, this is very rich, so you can count on it being enough for 8 to 10 people at least.*

To make peeling the cloves go quickly, crush each with the broad side of a heavy knife first; the papery outer peel will all but fall away. Or use a garlic peeler, which can be found in gourmet shops and mail-order catalogs. It looks like an oversized piece of plastic macaroni. You can spare the investment and improvise with one of those flat disks of rubber used to open stubborn jar lids. Wrap it around a garlic clove making a tube. Then press and roll it on the counter, and the rubber will scrub off the skin.

3 heads of garlic
3 cups milk
3 (2-ounce) cans flat anchovy fillets, drained
I cup extra-virgin olive oil
Freshly ground pepper

I. Separate the cloves of garlic and remove the skins. Place the peeled garlic in a large heavy saucepan. Add the milk and bring to a boil over medium heat. Reduce the heat to low and simmer, uncovered, until the garlic is tender and the milk is reduced to 1 cup, about 40 minutes.

2. Pour the reduced milk and the garlic into a food processor or blender. Add the anchovies and puree until smooth. With the machine on, slowly pour the oil through the feed tube. Season generously with pepper.

3. If the bagna cauda has cooled, reheat in a heavy saucepan over low heat. Serve in a small chafing dish, fondue pot, or other heatproof dish over a candle or Sterno flame.

Greek Mashed Potato Dip with Garlic and Walnuts

Makes about 1¼ cups

There are almost as many versions of this garlicky sauce, called skordalia in Greek, as there are Greek grandmothers and cooks. Some add body with potatoes; others use bread. Some add tartness with lemon juice; others opt for vinegar. Many enrich the mix with walnuts. All whip it together with olive oil—the fruitier, the better. I've opted for the full treatment, which means I add all of the above.

The proportions I've given below yield a fairly thick puree. To use it as a dip for raw vegetables or cooked artichokes, you may want to thin the sauce a bit with a little extra olive oil. It also makes a fabulous topping for fish cakes or grilled meaty fish.

1 medium baking potato (about 6 ounces)
3 slices day-old Italian bread, crusts removed
3 garlic cloves, smashed
½ cup walnut pieces
3 tablespoons fresh lemon juice
3 tablespoons red wine vinegar
¼ teaspoon salt
⅛ teaspoon sugar
¼ cup extra-virgin olive oil
Freshly ground pepper

I. Peel the potato and cut it into 1½-inch chunks. Bring a medium saucepan of salted water to a boil. Add the potato and cook until tender, 12 to 15 minutes. Drain well.

2. Soak the bread in a dish of warm water for about 2 minutes to soften. Remove the bread and squeeze out the water.

3. To mince the garlic, drop it through the feed tube of a food processor while the machine is on. Add the softened bread, cooked potato, walnuts, lemon juice, vinegar, salt, and sugar. Process until the mixture looks like fine crumbs. With the machine on, slowly add the oil through the feed tube until fully incorporated. Season with pepper and additional salt to taste. Serve the dip at room temperature.

Cucumber and Minted Yogurt Dip

Makes about 1¾ cups

This *refreshing dip is known as* tzatziki *in Greece. It's nice with toasted pita triangles or as a dipping sauce for grilled ground lamb skewers: Season ground lamb with salt, pepper, and oregano; form into 2-inch-long ovals around wooden skewers and grill over a fire or under a broiler. Also keep this cool dip in mind to serve with spicy food, especially Indian curries.*

1 medium cucumber, peeled
¼ teaspoon salt
1 cup plain yogurt
2 tablespoons chopped fresh mint
2 garlic cloves, peeled and minced
1 tablespoon extra-virgin olive oil
1 teaspoon fresh lemon juice

1. Cut the cucumber lengthwise in half and scoop out the seeds. Shred the cucumber on the large holes of a hand grater or in a food processor. Transfer the shredded cucumber to a strainer and toss with the salt. Let stand for at least 30 minutes, tossing once or twice.

2. Squeeze the cucumber in a clean kitchen towel to remove excess moisture. Place in a medium bowl.

3. Add the yogurt, mint, garlic, olive oil, and lemon juice. Stir to mix well. Season with additional salt to taste. Cover and refrigerate until serving time.

Black Olive and Dried Tomato Tapenade

While other bright flavors here take star billing, there's no mistaking the generous amount of garlic underneath. Salty and pungent, this is a tasty spread to use on Crostini (page 90) or to spread on sandwiches made with peasant-style bread. It's also a good dip for cauliflower florets, fennel or celery sticks, and baby carrots. A couple of tablespoons will transform a simple tuna salad into a Mediterranean delight.

Many markets now sell pitted Kalamata olives, but to pit the olives yourself quickly and easily: Crush the olives with the flat side of a heavy knife, as you would garlic before peeling it; then simply sort out the pits from the olives.

24 sun-dried tomato halves (not oil-packed), 2 ounces dry
3 garlic cloves, peeled and cut in half
½ cup Kalamata or other brine-cured imported black olives, pitted
½ (2-ounce) can flat anchovies (3 or 4 fillets), drained
3 tablespoons capers, drained
¼ cup extra-virgin olive oil
½ cup coarsely chopped fresh basil
1 tablespoon fresh lemon juice

1. With scissors, snip the sun-dried tomatoes into strips. Place them in a bowl with the garlic and cover with boiling water. Set aside for 30 minutes to soften; drain.

2. In a food processor or blender, combine the softened tomatoes and the garlic with the olives, anchovies, and capers. Process, stopping the machine occasionally to scrape the sides of the bowl, until finely chopped.

3. With the machine on, pour the olive oil through the feed tube and blend until incorporated. Add the basil and lemon juice and pulse just until the basil is finely chopped.

Best of the
Beans

When you think of bean dip, the first thing that probably comes to mind is a sprightly Southwestern blend. Why not? Fiery chiles, fragrant cumin, and pungent freshly chopped cilantro provide just the right boost to the blandness of beans. You'll find two variations of that popular version here. One is a pinto bean puree, zipped up with jalapeño peppers and taco sauce; the other a black bean dip, seasoned with Southwestern spices, enriched with melted Monterey Jack cheese, and garnished with fresh cilantro. But you'll also discover how well no-fat, high-carbohydrate, and high-fiber beans take to flavors from all around the world. Choose also from a classic Middle Eastern Hummus, chickpeas blended with lemon, garlic, and parsley, or an Asian Sesame Bean Spread, flavored with scallions, *omeboshi* (pickled plum) vinegar, and sesame oil. For almost any occasion, from Superbowl Sunday to a New Year's buffet, a simple Herbed Black-Eyed Pea Dip is the perfect choice.

All of these bean preparations are gutsy and will hold up well. For simplicity and speed, canned beans are suggested as an alternative to cooked beans throughout. If you opt for cooking dried beans, be sure to soak them overnight before boiling, so they will end up evenly softened and digestible.

Hummus

This *Middle Eastern blend of chickpeas (sometimes called garbanzo beans), tahini, lemon juice, and garlic, enriched with a little olive oil, is one of the all-time most popular bean dips. It pairs best with Herbed Pita Chips (page 88), but also makes a tempting dip for crudités. Try it also as a spread for a vegetarian sandwich.*

A few notes on the ingredients: Use flat-leaf parsley (also known as Italian parsley), because it has more flavor than the curly kind. Tahini, Middle Eastern sesame paste, can be found in Asian markets, in health food stores, and in supermarkets stocked with the Asian ingredients or next to the peanut butter—which makes a reasonable, if unorthodox, substitute.

2 garlic cloves, peeled
1½ cups cooked chickpeas or 1 (15½-ounce) can, rinsed and drained
¼ cup tahini (Middle Eastern sesame paste) or smooth peanut butter
3 tablespoons fresh lemon juice
2 tablespoons olive oil
¼ teaspoon ground cumin
¼ teaspoon salt
⅓ cup chopped flat-leaf parsley
Paprika

I. Mince the garlic by dropping it through the feed tube of a food processor or blender while the machine is on. Add the chickpeas, tahini, lemon juice, olive oil, cumin, and salt. Puree until smooth, stopping the machine once or twice to scrape down the sides of the bowl.

2. Add the parsley and pulse just until mixed. Season with additional salt to taste. Transfer to a bowl or small platter and dust the top with paprika. Serve at room temperature.

Ranch Rider Red Bean Dip

Makes 2 ½ cups

If you don't mind the taste of raw garlic and onion, skip Step 1, omit the oil, and mix all the ingredients in a food processor or blender. Or for something in between cooking and not, simply rinse the chopped onion for a few minutes in a strainer under very hot tap water to tame its raw bite. Tortilla chips, slices of jicama, and bell pepper strips would all make good dippers here.

I tablespoon olive oil
I small onion, chopped
2 garlic cloves, smashed
2 cups cooked red kidney beans or I (19-ounce) can, rinsed and drained
2 fresh jalapeño peppers or I (4-ounce) can chopped green chiles, drained
½ cup prepared taco sauce
¾ teaspoon ground coriander
¼ teaspoon salt

1. Combine the oil, onion, and garlic in a medium skillet. Set over medium heat and cook, stirring frequently, until the onion is softened and translucent, 3 to 5 minutes.

2. Scrape the contents of the skillet into a food processor or blender. Add the kidney beans, jalapeño peppers, taco sauce, ground coriander, and salt. Puree until smooth. Serve at room temperature.

Refried Black Bean Dip
with Melted Jack

Makes 2 cups

This is a spicy dip that tastes best when served warm. You can put it in a small bowl or fondue pot over a Sterno flame or serve it in a heavy earthenware bowl, which will hold the heat, and refill it as needed. Vary the spiciness level with the kind of chile peppers you choose. Jalapeños are best for moderate but pronounced heat; serranos are generally hotter, but typically Mexican. If cans of chopped green chiles are all you can find, use a 4-ounce can, drained, and add a dash of cayenne, since these are usually quite mild.

1 teaspoon chili powder
½ teaspoon ground cumin
1 tablespoon olive oil
1 small onion, chopped
2 garlic cloves, minced
1½ cups cooked black beans or 1 (15-ounce) can, rinsed and drained
1 medium tomato, chopped
2 pickled jalapeño peppers, chopped
¼ to ½ teaspoon salt
1 cup shredded Monterey Jack cheese
2 tablespoons cilantro leaves

1. Place the chili powder and cumin in a medium skillet, preferably non-stick, and toast over medium heat, stirring constantly, until fragrant, about 1 minute. Remove the spices to a small dish and set aside.

2. Add the olive oil, onion, and garlic to the skillet. Cook over medium heat, stirring frequently, until the onion is softened and translucent, 3 to 5 minutes.

3. Add the beans and mash about half of them against the side of the skillet with the back of a spoon. Blend in the tomato, jalapeño peppers, ¼ teaspoon salt, and the toasted spices. Cook, stirring often, for 5 minutes.

4. Stir in the cheese and continue to cook, stirring, until melted, about 1 minute. Taste and add the remaining ¼ teaspoon salt if you think it needs it. Remove from the heat and spoon into a serving dish. Garnish with the cilantro and serve at once.

Asian Sesame Bean Spread

Makes 2 cups

This dip has the clean, vivid taste that is so typical of good Asian cooking. It is best made with tiny pink adzuki beans and pungent, salty ume vinegar, made from pickled umeboshi plums. Both are available in Asian markets and in health food stores. If you substitute pinto beans and plain rice vinegar, more salt may be needed. Wonton Crisps (page 89) are a natural accompaniment.

1 garlic clove, smashed

2 scallions, cut into 2-inch lengths

2 cups cooked adzuki, small pink beans, or pinto beans, or 1 (15-ounce) can,
    rinsed and drained

½ cup coarsely chopped onion

1 tablespoon umeboshi or rice vinegar

¼ to ½ teaspoon salt

1 teaspoon Asian sesame oil

⅛ teaspoon hot pepper sauce

¼ cup cilantro leaves

I. Mince the garlic and scallions by dropping them through the feed tube of a food processor or blender while the machine is on.

2. Add the beans, onion, vinegar, ¼ teaspoon salt, sesame oil, hot sauce, and 3 tablespoons of the cilantro. Puree until smooth, stopping occasionally to scrape down the sides of the bowl.

3. Taste and season with the remaining salt if you think it is needed. Scrape the dip into a bowl and garnish with the remaining cilantro leaves. Serve at room temperature.

Herbed Black-Eyed Pea Dip

Makes 1 ⅔ cups

Here's a fresh-tasting, lightly seasoned preparation that makes a nice starter for a late brunch. Since tradition has it that black-eyed peas bring good luck to anyone who eats them on New Year's Day, don't forget this recipe when that holiday rolls around.

If you make this from scratch with thawed frozen or fresh black-eyed peas, cook them as directed on the package label. Canned peas need only be drained into a colander and rinsed under running water. A bowl of Chutney Ham Spread (page 30) and large corn chips or crisp pita triangles along with this dip will practically make a meal.

1 garlic clove, smashed
⅓ cup flat-leaf parsley leaves
1½ cups cooked black-eyed peas or 1 (15½-ounce) can, rinsed and
    drained
2 tablespoons fresh lemon juice
2 tablespoons olive oil
½ teaspoon dried tarragon
½ teaspoon salt
¼ teaspoon freshly ground pepper
Parsley sprigs, for garnish

1. Mince the garlic by dropping it through the feed tube of a food processor or blender while the machine is on. Add the parsley leaves and pulse to chop.

2. Add the black-eyed peas, lemon juice, olive oil, tarragon, salt, and pepper. Puree until smooth, stopping to scrape down the sides of the bowl once or twice.

3. Spoon into a serving dish and garnish with parsley sprigs. Serve at room temperature.

Rosemary and White Bean Spread
with Toasted Walnuts

Lush with rosemary and walnuts, slightly tart with a hint of balsamic vinegar, this lovely spread is a natural on Crostini (page 90) or on pita wedges. It's lovely paired with sweet red peppers and makes a great sandwich spread on semolina bread and topped with arugula. Or put out a pot of this smooth bean spread with a basket of pencil-thin bread sticks—called gristini in Italy—and serve a bottle of chilled Soave white wine.

1/2 cup walnut pieces or pine nuts

1 (20-ounce) can white beans, drained, or 2 cups cooked white beans

1 garlic clove, minced

1/2 cup extra-virgin olive oil

1 tablespoon balsamic vinegar

1 tablespoon chopped fresh rosemary or 1 teaspoon dried, crumbled

1/4 teaspoon salt

1/8 teaspoon freshly ground pepper

1. Preheat the oven to 375°F. Spread out the walnuts on a small baking sheet and toast in the oven, stirring once or twice, until the nuts are lightly browned and fragrant, 7 to 10 minutes. Watch carefully, because nuts burn quickly.

2. In a food processor, combine the drained beans with the toasted walnuts and garlic. Pulse until coarsely pureed.

3. With the machine on, add the olive oil through the feed tube. Add the vinegar, rosemary, salt, and pepper and puree until almost smooth. Season with additional salt and pepper to taste before serving. Serve at room temperature.

Variation

White Bean Dip with Sun-Dried Tomatoes and Basil: Omit the nuts and skip Step 1. Increase the garlic to 2 cloves and add 8 (oil-packed) sun-dried tomato halves in Step 2. Substitute 2 tablespoons chopped fresh basil for the rosemary.

Especially Hot and
Sassy

Some like it hot, and some like it hotter. Chips and chiles are seemingly a match made in heaven. With this selection of spicy dips and spreads, you'll be able to please everyone who loves their food on the flaming side. There's a range of heat, of course, depending upon the power source: from mildly spicy jalapeño peppers and the slightly more piquant serranos to fiery crushed hot pepper flakes and smoky hot chipotle chiles, which are dried ripe jalapeños. Where a recipe calls simply for hot pepper sauce, feel free to adjust the heat and flavor slightly by choosing your favorite brand.

You'll find chipotle chiles dried in packages with the other specialty produce in the grocery store or canned in adobo sauce in the Asian or Mexican section. The canned ones are easiest to use, and they'll turn whatever dish you add them to a delightful terra-cotta color. Dried chipotles must be stemmed, seeded, and soaked in warm water to soften for about 30 minutes before use.

One especially incendiary dip, Caribbean Jerk Barbecue Sauce, specifies a Scotch Bonnet pepper or as an alternative, a habanero, two of the hottest chiles on the planet. Both should be treated with respect and restraint. Once you get past the heat, though, you'll discover the delight of their deep, complex flavors. If you enjoy the flavor, but want to dampen the fire, prick the pepper all over with a fork (watch out for the oils that may spray from the skin; they're hot, too) and add the pepper whole, in one piece, to the finished sauce. When you're ready to serve, just pluck it out. You'll get an infusion of the taste without the full temperature.

The heat from any chile can be tamed somewhat by removing the seeds and ribs (the pale inside membranes that divide the peppers into segments) before chopping them. This is where most of the capsaicin, the compound that carries the heat, resides. If you're particularly sensitive, thin rubber gloves will prevent irritation from the oils in the pepper. Be sure to wash hands, and gloves, after working with chiles to prevent the volatile oils from spreading to other foods—and to other body parts, such as your eyes!

Spicy Guacamole with Cilantro and Tomato

Makes about 1 cup

To get the most avocado flavor, use only a ripe fruit that will yield to gentle pressure, like a peach. Those grown in California with the pebbly black or dark green skins, often labeled "Hass," have the richest flavor and creamiest texture. The easiest way to open an avocado is to use a heavy sharp knife and cut the avocado lengthwise in half. Twist the two halves in opposite directions to separate them. Hold the half with the pit in the palm of your hand and carefully whack the pit with a knife so that it sticks into the pit. Twist the knife and lift it out. Then use a spoon to scoop the avocado from its skin.

1 ripe avocado, preferably Hass or other pebbly skinned variety
2 tablespoons fresh lime juice
1 tablespoon finely chopped white onion
1 to 2 serrano or jalapeño peppers, minced
1/3 cup coarsely chopped fresh cilantro
1 small tomato, seeded and finely chopped
1/4 teaspoon salt
Hot pepper sauce

1. Cut the avocado in half, remove the pit, and scoop the avocado into a medium bowl. Using a potato masher or a large fork, mash the avocado coarsely so there are still some lumps.

2. Add the lime juice, onion, serrano or jalapeño peppers, cilantro, tomato, and salt. Stir to mix.

3. Taste and add as much hot sauce as you like if needed for heat. Serve at room temperature.

Note: If you don't serve the guacamole at once, to retard discoloration, press the avocado pit into the dip, then cover with a sheet of plastic wrap pressed down to cover the surface. Just before serving, discard the pit and stir up the guacamole.

Asian Spiced Eggplant Spread

Makes 2 1/4 cups

Baba ganoush meets the Pacific Rim in this updated classic. For added smoky flavor when weather and time permit, consider lighting the barbecue grill or broiler and charring the skin of the eggplants, garlic, and scallion before proceeding with the recipe. Herbed Pita Chips (page 88) or Wonton Crisps (page 89) are the natural accompaniment to this excellent dip.

I tablespoon sesame seeds
2 medium eggplants, scrubbed (leave the skin on) and cut crosswise into
     1/4-inch slices
2 tablespoons olive oil
I garlic clove, smashed
I (1-inch) piece of fresh ginger, peeled and sliced
I scallion, cut into 2-inch pieces
2 tablespoons soy sauce
2 tablespoons rice vinegar
I tablespoon sugar
I teaspoon Asian sesame oil
1/2 to I teaspoon crushed hot red pepper flakes, to taste
1/2 teaspoon salt
3/4 cup cilantro leaves

I. Preheat the oven to 450°F. Meanwhile, toast the sesame seeds in a small dry skillet over low heat, stirring constantly, until golden and fragrant, about 5 minutes. Set aside.

2. Lightly oil 2 baking sheets and arrange the eggplant slices on them in a single layer. Brush both sides of each slice lightly with a little olive oil. Roast without turning until fork-tender, 30 to 35 minutes. Let cool, then coarsely chop the eggplant.

3. With the machine on, drop the garlic, ginger, and scallion into a food processor to mince them. Add the roasted eggplant, soy sauce, vinegar, sugar, sesame oil, hot pepper, salt, and half the cilantro. Puree until smooth. Spoon the spread into a serving dish and garnish with the remaining cilantro and the toasted sesame seeds.

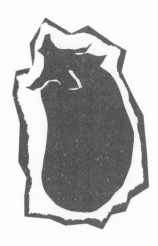

Caribbean Jerk Barbecue Sauce

Makes about 2 cups

Don't let the long list of ingredients here scare you off. With the exception of the mango and the Scotch bonnet pepper, which can now be found in many supermarkets pretty much year-round, everything is widely available and probably already in your kitchen cupboard. All of these ingredients help to build the complexity of the flavors that is the soul of island cooking.

In the Caribbean, the fresh ingredients would typically be smoked before assembling, but the flavor is delightful without that laborious step. I've suggested a bit of liquid smoke to add a hint of wood without the work. Serve this sauce as a dip with chips of any kind. Plantain chips go particularly well with it. It also makes a great sauce for chicken wings and spareribs, whether you dip them in or brush it on.

Note: If the fiery hot Scotch bonnet pepper is not available, substitute 2 serrano chile peppers.

1 medium green bell pepper, coarsely chopped

1 medium red bell pepper, coarsely chopped

2 tablespoons tomato paste

2 garlic cloves, peeled and halved

1 ripe mango or papaya, peeled and seed(s) removed

1 small onion, coarsely chopped

1 Scotch bonnet pepper, halved and seeded

¼ cup plus 2 tablespoons cider vinegar

½ cup packed dark brown sugar

2 tablespoons molasses

2 tablespoons Dijon mustard

1 tablespoon ground cinnamon

1½ teaspoons ground cumin

1 teaspoon dried thyme leaves

¼ teaspoon salt

½ teaspoon liquid smoke (optional)

1. Combine all the ingredients except the liquid smoke in a large stainless steel saucepan. Stir in 1 cup water. Bring to a boil over high heat. Reduce the heat to low, cover, and simmer 1 hour, stirring occasionally. Remove from the heat and let cool.

2. Puree the sauce in a blender or food processor. Strain through a fine sieve. Stir in the liquid smoke if you want to use it. Season with additional salt to taste. If made ahead, transfer the sauce to a lidded jar and refrigerate for up to a week.

Peanut Dipping Sauce

Makes about 1 cup

This is the sauce served with Indonesian and Thai satays— skewered and grilled strips of chicken, lamb, chicken livers, or beef. In Indonesia a similar sauce is used as a salad dressing for Gado Gado, a sumptuous main-course salad of steamed and raw vegetables, such as potatoes, carrots, cabbage wedges, cauliflower florets, green beans, tomatoes, and bean sprouts, all of which would also make an interesting variation on the standard crudités plate.

1 (½-inch) piece of fresh ginger, peeled and sliced
1 garlic clove, smashed
½ cup smooth peanut butter
2 tablespoons fresh lime juice
1 to 1½ tablespoons soy sauce
1 tablespoon rice vinegar
1 tablespoon brown sugar
½ to 1 teaspoon crushed hot red pepper flakes

1. Mince the ginger and garlic by dropping them through the feed tube of a food processor while the machine is on. Add the peanut butter, lime juice, 1 tablespoon of the soy sauce, the vinegar, brown sugar, and ½ teaspoon of the hot pepper. Blend well.

2. Taste the sauce and add more soy sauce or hot pepper to your taste. Add 1 to 2 tablespoons hot water to thin to dipping consistency and blend again. Serve at room temperature.

3. If the dip thickens upon standing, thin with a little more hot water.

Chipotle-Lime Cream

Makes 1 ½ cups

This is a good illustration of how refined and feisty can make a loving marriage. The peacemaker is the whipped cream folded in at the end. It both mellows the flavor and lightens the texture. If you're in a hurry, though, you can just double the sour cream and omit the heavy cream. This spicy, tart dip is especially good with fried clams, fried calamari, or grilled vegetables.

1 canned chipotle chile in adobo sauce, minced (about 1 ½ teaspoons)

½ cup sour cream

Grated zest of 1 lime

1 tablespoon fresh lime juice

¼ teaspoon sugar

¼ teaspoon salt

¼ cup heavy cream

1. In a small bowl, combine the chipotle and any adobo sauce that clings to it with the sour cream and the lime zest. Stir to mix well. Cover and refrigerate for at least 30 minutes to allow the flavors to blend.

2. Stir the lime juice, sugar, and salt into the chipotle-sour cream base. In another bowl, using an electric hand mixer or a wire whisk, beat the heavy cream until stiff peaks form. Fold the beaten cream into the chipotle-sour cream until blended. Serve at once or cover and refrigerate for up to 2 hours.

East-West Wasabi and Mustard Mayonnaise

Makes about ¾ cup

Directions are given here for making your own mayonnaise in a food processor, but if you prefer, you can skip this step. Just stir the lemon juice, toasted mustard seeds, mustard, and wasabi powder into ¾ cup of your favorite brand of bottled mayonnaise. Once you taste the difference that homemade makes, however—especially if you use olive oil—I think you'll be convinced it is worth the small bother.

Wasabi is the green paste that brings sushi eaters to tears. It is actually the root of a plant related to horseradish. You'll find it packaged as a powder in small cans next to the other Asian ingredients in the supermarket.

This potent mayonnaise is particularly good as a dip with crudités or cooked shrimp or as a sauce drizzled over poached or grilled salmon.

1 tablespoon mustard seeds
1 egg
1 tablespoon fresh lemon juice
1 tablespoon Dijon mustard
1 tablespoon wasabi powder
⅔ cup olive or peanut oil

1. Place the mustard seeds in a small dry skillet and toast them over medium-low heat, stirring constantly, until they darken and pop, 2 to 3 minutes. Transfer to a small dish and set aside.

2. In a food processor or blender, combine the egg, lemon juice, Dijon mustard, and wasabi powder. Blend briefly. With the machine on, slowly pour in the oil in a thin stream, processing until fully incorporated.

3. Transfer the mayonnaise to a small bowl. Stir in the toasted mustard seeds. Let stand for 30 minutes before serving to allow the flavors to develop. If made ahead, cover and refrigerate for up to 1 day; if stored longer, the wasabi will begin to lose its liveliness.

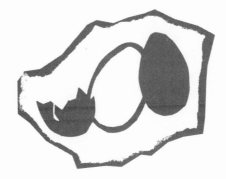

Santa Fe Chile and Plum Tomato Dipping Sauce

Makes about 2 cups

Spoon some of this robust dip into a small dish and serve it along with a platter of sliced jicama and mango sprinkled with lime or simply with a basket of freshly baked tortilla chips. If you want more chile flavor and less heat, use guajillo chiles; for more heat, look for Anaheim chiles. Thinned with a little chicken broth, this also makes a good red sauce for enchiladas.

2 ounces dried red chiles, such as New Mexico or ancho
1 pound plum tomatoes, cut in half
3 garlic cloves, smashed
1 tablespoon olive oil
1 teaspoon ground cumin
½ teaspoon dried oregano
½ teaspoon salt
¼ teaspoon sugar
Cayenne, optional

1. Preheat the broiler. Grease a baking sheet and set it aside. Stem and seed the chiles and tear them into long, wide strips. Place them in a bowl and cover with boiling water. Set aside to soften, about 15 minutes. Drain and discard the soaking liquid.

2. Meanwhile, place the tomatoes cut-sides down on the prepared baking sheet. Broil until the skins are charred, about 5 minutes. Remove and let cool.

3. Mince the garlic by dropping it through the feed tube of a food processor or blender while the machine is on. Stop the motor and add the softened chiles. Puree until smooth. Strain through a fine sieve.

4. Heat the oil in a large saucepan over medium heat. Add the strained chile puree, the cumin, oregano, salt, and sugar. (Be careful because the sauce may splatter when it hits the hot oil.) Bring to a boil, stirring often. Reduce the heat to low and simmer, stirring constantly, until the sauce darkens and thickens, 10 to 15 minutes. Season with additional salt and/or sugar to taste. If the sauce doesn't have enough heat for your taste, spike it with some cayenne.

Artfully
Elegant

Elegant means different things to different people. What distinguishes a dish
from everyday fare might be the luxuriousness—read costliness—of the ingredients, which make it seem like a splurge, or the presentation, which dresses it up.
Or the appetizer might be so rich that indulging in it makes the party a special
occasion.

Smoked salmon, caviar, and crab are a few of the more extravagant items
called for here, but luckily, dips and spreads allow ways to cut corners. Because
everything is mashed up, perfection is not necessary. When purchasing smoked
salmon for a dip or spread, look for ends and trimmings, which are much less
expensive than whole slices. Beluga or sevruga caviar by itself is an immense
treat, but when blended with onion, sour cream, and what-have-you, lumpfish or
whitefish caviar or salmon roe might serve just as well, at a small fraction of the
price tag.

A selection of recipes chosen from this chapter would make a sumptuous
cocktail party buffet. They're a little special, but none require much of a time com-
mitment or last-minute handling. As an added bonus, most of these dips and
spreads travel well and will be welcomed anytime you're asked to bring an hors
d'oeuvre to a potluck party.

Dilled Smoked Salmon Spread

Makes about 1½ cups

Although this sophisticated spread can be thrown together in mere moments, it's elegant enough to offer to your most discerning guests on the most important of occasions. Serve it with crackers, toast points, party pumpernickel, or Melba toasts. Besides providing a great start to a fancy dinner, the spread makes a tasty bagel topper at brunch.

6 ounces smoked salmon, thinly sliced

6 ounces cream cheese, softened

¼ cup sour cream

1½ tablespoons fresh lemon juice

½ teaspoon freshly ground pepper

¼ cup minced fresh chives or 1 tablespoon chopped scallion greens

2 tablespoons chopped fresh dill

1. With a large stainless steel knife, finely dice or chop the salmon. Alternatively, place it in a food processor and pulse to finely chop, but do not puree to a paste.

2. In a medium bowl, beat the cream cheese with a wooden spoon until light and fluffy. Blend in the sour cream, lemon juice, and pepper.

3. Add the smoked salmon, chives, and dill. Stir until evenly combined. If not used when made, cover and refrigerate until serving time. The spread will keep well for up to 3 days.

Potted Smoked Trout

Makes about I cup

Melba toasts, toasted triangles of white or whole-grain bread, party rye, or crackers are all excellent as bases for this sumptuous spread. It's also excellent on spears of cucumber or Belgian endive and, not surprisingly, on toasted bagels.

4 ounces boneless smoked trout

3 ounces cream cheese, at room temperature

2 tablespoons unsalted butter, at room temperature

1 tablespoon fresh lemon juice

1½ teaspoons minced shallot or white of scallion

1 teaspoon prepared white horseradish, drained

2 teaspoons chopped fresh dill or ½ teaspoon dried

¼ teaspoon salt

Freshly ground pepper

1. Remove any skin from the trout. If the fish has come on the bone, gently lift it up and most of the meat will come off in one piece. Flake the smoked trout, being sure there are no hidden small bones.

2. Place the trout in a food processor. Add the cream cheese, butter, lemon juice, shallot, horseradish, and dill. Pulse until fairly smooth. Season with the salt and generously with pepper to taste.

3. Pack into a crock, cover, and refrigerate until serving time. The spread will keep well for up to 5 days.

Caviar Dip

Stretch pricey caviar by blending it with other ingredients that make it go a lot further and serving it as a dip. Either use tiny, firm red or golden lumpfish or whitefish caviar or the soft, larger pink salmon roe, depending on your taste. Or mix two together to vary the flavor and texture. Melba toasts or triangles of homemade toast, made from sandwich bread trimmed of its crust, are good for spreading. Spears of Belgian endive make excellent dippers.

6 ounces whipped cream cheese, at room temperature
½ cup sour cream
1 tablespoon fresh lemon juice
2 teaspoons grated onion
2 tablespoons minced fresh chives or scallion greens
2 ounces red lumpfish or golden whitefish caviar, and/or salmon roe

1. In a small bowl, mix the cream cheese with the sour cream and lemon juice until well blended. Stir in the onion and 1 tablespoon of the chives. Gently fold all but ½ teaspoon of the caviar into the cream.

2. Spoon the dip into a serving dish. Garnish with the reserved chives and caviar. If not serving at once, cover and refrigerate.

Chicken Liver Pâté with Calvados and Thyme

Makes about 2 cups

If *you use a food processor or blender, this perennial favorite can be whipped up in a flash. You won't actually taste the apples, but they add body and lightness and reduce the percentage of calories from fat. The velvety texture and rich flavor of chicken livers marry beautifully with a pitcher of martinis or Manhattans, with Sauternes or a late-harvest Riesling, dry red wine, or simply a glass of sparkling water with lime.*

2 tablespoons unsalted butter
I small onion, chopped
2 tart apples, peeled, cored, and cubed
2 garlic cloves, peeled and minced
I pound chicken livers, trimmed
2 tablespoons Calvados or apple brandy
½ teaspoon dried thyme leaves
I teaspoon salt
¼ cup heavy cream
Freshly ground pepper

I. In a medium skillet, melt the butter over medium heat. When the foam subsides, add the onion, apples, and garlic. Cook, stirring occasionally, until the onion is soft and translucent, 5 to 8 minutes.

2. Add the chicken livers and cook, tossing, until they are no longer pink, 8 to 10 minutes. Add the Calvados, thyme, and salt. Remove from the heat and transfer to a food processor or blender. Add the cream and puree until smooth. Season generously with pepper to taste.

3. Spoon into a serving dish, cover with plastic wrap, and refrigerate for up to 3 days until ready to serve.

Brandied Mushroom Pâté

Makes 1 ½ cups

Turn *to this page when you want a truly elegant vegetarian spread that everyone will enjoy. The earthy flavor goes particularly well with rye crackers. For inveterate meat eaters, spread the mushroom pâté on rye toast points and top with lean roast beef.*

1 pound white button mushrooms
4 tablespoons unsalted butter
6 shallots, finely chopped
1 tablespoon flour
2 tablespoons Cognac or brandy
3 tablespoons heavy cream
2 teaspoons chopped fresh tarragon or ¾ teaspoon dried
1 teaspoon salt
½ teaspoon freshly ground pepper
1 teaspoon fresh lemon juice
¼ cup chopped fresh parsley

I. Trim the ends off the mushroom stems; quarter the mushrooms. Place half the mushrooms at a time in a food processor and pulse to chop finely. Squeeze the chopped mushrooms in a clean kitchen towel to remove as much liquid as possible.

2. Melt the butter in a large skillet, preferably nonstick, over medium-high heat. When the foam subsides, add the mushrooms and shallots and sauté until all the mushrooms give up their liquid and it boils off, 5 to 7 minutes.

3. Sprinkle on the flour, reduce the heat to medium, and cook, stirring, 30 to 60 seconds. Pour in the Cognac and let it bubble up. Add the cream, tarragon, salt, and pepper. Cook, stirring, until thickened, about 1 minute.

4. Remove from the heat and stir in the lemon juice and parsley. Pack the pâté into a crock or a lightly oiled 2-cup mold or bowl. Cover and refrigerate until chilled, at least 3 hours or up to 2 days. If molded, invert to release onto a platter before serving. Serve slightly chilled or at room temperature.

Romesco Sauce

Toasted almonds, roasted garlic, and sweet peppers form the base of this delectable brick-red dip. Since it contains no mayonnaise or meat, it stands up well at room temperature and is a great choice for a buffet or party. Because the sauce holds its flavor well in the refrigerator for up to 5 days, it's one of those handy entertaining recipes you can get out of the way ahead of time.

3 medium red bell peppers
1 large plum tomato
1 cup whole natural almonds
6 garlic cloves
1 ½ teaspoons cumin seeds
1 ½ tablespoons fresh lemon juice
½ teaspoon oregano
½ teaspoon salt
½ teaspoon crushed hot red pepper flakes
¼ teaspoon freshly ground black pepper
¼ cup extra-virgin olive oil
⅔ cup hot water

1. Preheat the oven to 475°F. Cut the peppers lengthwise in half and remove the stems and seeds. Place them skin side up on a baking sheet and roast without turning for 20 minutes, or until the skins are charred. Remove the peppers and set aside. Reduce the oven temperature to 375°.

2. Cut the plum tomato in half and squeeze gently to remove the seeds. Place on the baking sheet. Spread out the almonds on the baking sheet and in a separate spot, add the garlic cloves in their skins. Roast, stirring the almonds and turning the garlic cloves once or twice, until the nuts are toasted and fragrant and the garlic is beginning to soften and turn golden, 8 to 10 minutes.

3. While the ingredients are roasting, remove the skins from the peppers and place them in a food processor. In a small dry skillet, toast the cumin seeds over medium heat, shaking the pan, until the seeds darken slightly and smell fragrant, 2 to 3 minutes. Add to the processor.

4. When they're roasted, add the almonds, tomato, and cumin seeds to the processor. Squeeze the garlic cloves from their skins and add to the processor. Add the lemon juice, oregano, salt, hot pepper, and black pepper. Process until almost smooth.

5. With the machine on, add first the oil and then the hot water through the feed tube. Puree until smooth. Taste and season with additional salt, hot pepper, and black pepper to taste. Store this dip in a covered container in the refrigerator but serve it at room temperature.

Hot Crab and Artichoke Spread

Makes about 3 ½ cups

Hot appetizers are welcomed heartily by guests, and that's one of the reasons this classic has never gone out of style. The aroma alone is sensational. Serve it with crackers or toast points.

1 (14-ounce) can artichoke hearts
½ cup grated Parmesan cheese
1 (8-ounce) package cream cheese, softened
¼ cup mayonnaise
2 small garlic cloves, minced
½ teaspoon freshly ground black pepper
½ teaspoon Worcestershire sauce
⅛ teaspoon cayenne
½ pound fresh or thawed frozen crabmeat, well drained and patted dry
1 tablespoon fresh lemon juice

1. Preheat the oven to 400°F. Drain the artichoke hearts. Squeeze them in a clean kitchen towel to remove as much liquid as possible. Reserve 1 tablespoon of the Parmesan cheese.

2. In a food processor, combine the remaining Parmesan cheese with the artichoke hearts, cream cheese, mayonnaise, garlic, black pepper, Worcestershire sauce, and cayenne. Puree until smooth.

3. Pick over the crabmeat to remove any bits of shell or cartilage. Add the crabmeat and lemon juice to the artichoke puree and pulse just until mixed. Pour into a 1½-quart gratin or shallow baking dish. Sprinkle the reserved 1 tablespoon Parmesan cheese over the top.

4. Bake 20 to 25 minutes, or until the top is golden. Let stand about 10 minutes to cool and set slightly. Serve warm.

Green Olive and Walnut Pesto

Makes about 1½ cups

While we usually think of pesto as a basil sauce, in fact, the Italian word actually means "paste," and these days pesto comes in many flavors. Typically the blend is made with strong tastes and enough texture to add interest. This saucy spread, based on green olives and toasted walnuts, is especially good on Crostini (page 90) or with bread sticks or simple crackers. It also doubles deliciously as a pasta topping. To chop up all the ingredients, a food processor works best here. If you use a blender, you'll have better luck making the pesto in batches.

½ cup walnut pieces
1 cup pitted green olives, preferably Sicilian
1 cup flat-leaf parsley, tough stems removed
6 scallions, cut into 2-inch pieces
3 tablespoons fresh lemon juice
¼ teaspoon crushed hot red pepper flakes
⅓ cup olive oil

1. Preheat the oven to 325°F. Spread out the walnuts in a small baking dish. Toast in the oven, shaking the pan once or twice, until the nuts are lightly browned and fragrant, 5 to 7 minutes. Transfer to a plate and let cool.

2. In a food processor, combine the olives, toasted walnuts, parsley, scallions, lemon juice, and hot pepper. Pulse, scraping the sides of the bowl occasionally, until the mixture is very finely chopped.

3. With the machine on, slowly pour the olive oil through the feed tube until incorporated. Serve the pesto at room temperature.

Cheddar
and Better

Cheese comes in an astonishing variety of flavors, from the mildest cream cheese to the distinctive tang of a soft young goat cheese, from the full-bodied nuttiness of aged Cheddar to the pungent bite of Roquefort and other blue cheeses. It's one of the all-time most popular appetizer foods, whether set out in a wedge on its own or used as the base for other hors d'oeuvres, most notably, as here, in a delectable variety of dips and spreads.

Recipes range from the casual, such as Austrian Cheese Spread with Caraway and Anchovies, to the sophisticated, Party Roquefort Cheese Cake, for example. Some even improve if made ahead. And any one of several would make a delightful small meal or picnic, enjoyed with a salad, a loaf of bread, and a piece of fruit—not to speak of a glass of wine.

Sherried Cheddar and Blue Cheese Spread

Dry sherry, with its delicate nutty overtones, adds a touch of sweetness and toasty over-tones that I think are marvelous with Cheddar, but it can be replaced with port or, if you prefer, milk or cream for a nonalcoholic blend. Adjust the pungency of the spread with the cheeses you choose. Generally, the older the Cheddar, the sharper it tastes. Also Roquefort is a salty, very pungent cheese, while Danish blue, Wisconsin blue, and bleu d'Auvergne are milder and a little sweeter.

For looks here, I opt for orange Cheddar. The color comes from annatto, a natur-al seed, which adds color with little or no flavor. Because of the alcohol here, this is a spread you can make well in advance and keep in a covered crock in your refrigerator.

½ pound sharp Cheddar, finely shredded
¼ pound blue cheese, finely crumbled
1 (3-ounce) package cream cheese, softened
2 tablespoons Worcestershire sauce
1 teaspoon powdered mustard
¼ cup dry sherry

In a food processor, combine all the ingredients and blend until smooth, stopping the machine to scrape the sides of the bowl once or twice. Pack into a crock to serve. To store, cover and refrigerate for up to 2 weeks. The flavor of the spread will mellow as it ages.

Herbed Garlic Cheese Spread

Makes about 1 ¼ cups

Y*ou have to make your own yogurt cheese for this recipe, but it's extremely simple to do. All that's required is a little forethought to allow time for draining. The yogurt contributes a tartness and fresh taste for which there is no substitute. With the mix of garlic and herbs below, this savory spread tastes a lot like Boursin.*

Yogurt Cheese (recipe follows)
3 ounces mild soft white goat cheese, softened
1 tablespoon chopped fresh parsley
1 ½ teaspoons fresh thyme leaves or ½ teaspoon dried
1 teaspoon minced fresh rosemary or ¼ teaspoon dried, crumbled
1 garlic clove, crushed through a press
½ teaspoon salt
¼ teaspoon freshly ground pepper

In a food processor, combine all the ingredients. Whirl briefly to mix well. Transfer to a bowl, cover, and refrigerate for at least 2 hours to allow the flavors to develop. This spread will keep well in the refrigerator for up to 5 days.

Yogurt Cheese   Makes a scant ½ cup

Place a large coffee filter in a sieve or line the sieve with several layers of dampened cheesecloth. Place the sieve over a bowl. Spoon 1 cup plain yogurt into the sieve; cover and refrigerate, stirring occasionally, until the yogurt is thick and as much of the liquid whey as possible has drained out, at least 6 hours or overnight.

Party Roquefort Cheese Cake

If you're wondering how a 9-inch-diameter cake can serve two dozen or more, keep in mind that this savory cheese cake is rich and strongly flavored. With its crisp walnut crust, a thin sliver is heavenly and goes a long way.

3 slices of firm-textured white bread
½ cup walnut pieces
2 tablespoons butter, melted
2 tablespoons Cognac or brandy
¼ teaspoon salt
½ cup milk
3 large eggs
1 envelope (¼ ounce) unflavored gelatin
2 (8-ounce) packages cream cheese, softened
½ pound Roquefort or other blue cheese
1 teaspoon Worcestershire sauce
3 tablespoons minced fresh chives or scallion greens
1 cup heavy cream

1. Preheat the oven to 300°F. Tear the bread into pieces and place in a food processor. Pulse a few times. Add the walnuts and pulse until the bread is ground to crumbs and the nuts are finely chopped. Transfer to a bowl and stir in the melted butter, Cognac, and salt until the crumbs are evenly moistened. Press onto the bottom and 1 inch up the side of a 9-inch springform pan. Bake 15 minutes, or until the crust is golden brown. Remove from the oven and let cool.

2. For the filling, heat the milk over medium-low heat until small bubbles appear around the side of the pan. Beat the eggs in a small bowl. Whisk a little of the scalded milk into the eggs to warm them; then whisk the warmed eggs into the remaining hot milk. Cook, stirring constantly, until the custard thickens, about 5 minutes. It should register 160°F. on an instant-reading thermometer. Remove from the heat.

3. Soften the gelatin in $\frac{1}{2}$ cup cold water for 1 minute. Add to the hot custard and stir until dissolved. Scrape the custard into a medium bowl. Add the cream cheese and Roquefort and stir until evenly blended. Stir in the Worcestershire and chives. Let cool slightly.

4. In a medium bowl, beat the cream until it forms soft peaks. Fold the whipped cream into the cheese custard base. Pour into the prepared crust and refrigerate until chilled and set, at least 3 hours or overnight. To serve, cut into very thin wedges.

Sun-Dried Tomato and
Goat Cheese Spread with Fresh Basil

Makes about 2 cups

Pretty in pink. *That's how to describe this beauty. Serve it with melba toast or spread on a slice of grainy bread and top with arugula and a drizzle of olive oil for a light lunch or snack. Thin with a little milk or cream to turn it into a dip for raw or lightly cooked vegetables, grilled chicken, pork, or shrimp. It would also make an interesting base for pizza.*

It doesn't matter if you use oil-packed or desiccated sun-dried tomatoes here. Just drain the oil-packed ones or soak the dried ones in hot water for about 20 minutes to soften before using.

½ cup fresh basil leaves
10 to 12 sun-dried tomato halves
2 garlic cloves, smashed
8 ounces soft white goat cheese, at room temperature
6 ounces cream cheese, at room temperature
¾ teaspoon herbes de Provence or ½ teaspoon dried thyme and ¼ teaspoon
      dried rosemary
Freshly ground pepper

1. Pulse the basil in a food processor to chop. Remove and reserve 1 tablespoon. Add the dried tomatoes to the processor. With the machine on, drop the garlic through the feed tube and process to mince.

2. Add the goat cheese, cream cheese, and herbes de Provence. Puree until smooth. Season with pepper to taste.

3. Scrape into a serving dish and garnish with the reserved chopped basil. Serve slightly chilled or at room temperature.

Austrian Cheese Spread with Caraway and Anchovies

Makes 1½ cups

This simple-to-make spread is also known as Liptauer cheese, and it's popular in Austria and Hungary where it is made with sheep's milk cheese. This blend is a classic and for good reason, as you'll find when you watch it disappear. It's pungent and resembles the muted color of a Danube sunset in winter. Note: The anchovies are very subtle here. They add saltiness and a complexity of flavor, but if you don't tell, no one will know they're here.

1 (8-ounce) package cream cheese, softened

4 tablespoons unsalted butter, softened

2 teaspoons anchovy paste or 2 flat anchovy fillets

1 scallion, finely chopped

1½ teaspoons paprika

1 teaspoon capers, drained

½ teaspoon caraway seeds

½ teaspoon Worcestershire sauce

Place all the ingredients in a blender or food processor and puree until smooth, stopping the machine to scrape down the sides of the bowl once or twice. Transfer to a small bowl, cover, and refrigerate until serving time.

Chile con Queso

*T*he *color of adobe huts fills the towns where this dip originated. It must be served warm. This may be just the recipe to resurrect that fondue pot or chafing dish tucked away in the attic. Start with prepared salsa, choosing mild, medium, or hot, according to your preference, or use the Fresh Tomato Salsa on page 9.*

I cup tomato salsa
½ pound mild orange Cheddar cheese, shredded
I tablespoon all-purpose flour
¼ to ½ teaspoon crushed hot red pepper flakes, or more to taste

I. Spoon the salsa into a small saucepan and heat it over medium heat just to boiling.

2. Meanwhile, toss the cheese with the flour until evenly mixed. Gradually add to the hot salsa by handfuls, stirring until it melts. Do not allow the mixture to boil, or the cheese will become stringy and separate.

3. Season with hot pepper to taste. Transfer to a fondue pot, small chafing dish, or flameproof dish. Keep warm over a candle or Sterno.

Chips, Crisps, and Other
Dippers

Sure you can open a bag of chips. And why not? They are eminently convenient and there are so many different varieties: corn, tortilla, potato, plantain, and even root vegetable chips in all kinds of colors. But here are four dippers to turn to when homemade taste is essential—or when you forget to pick up a bag of store-bought.

Herbed Pita Chips

Makes 96

Depending on whether you start with white, whole wheat, or onion-flavored pita bread, this recipe can take on different temperaments. After baking, cool the chips completely before storing in a resealable plastic bag. They'll stay crisp for up to two days.

I (12-ounce) package whole wheat, white, or onion pita bread, about 7 inches in diameter

2 sticks (8 ounces) unsalted butter, softened

3 garlic cloves, crushed through a press

¼ cup chopped fresh herbs, such as thyme, parsley, mint, rosemary, sage, or a mixture

½ teaspoon coarse (kosher) salt

I. Preheat the oven to 325°F. Gently separate each pita bread to split into 2 thin rounds where they naturally separate.

2. In a small bowl, combine the softened butter with the garlic, herbs, and salt. Spread the seasoned butter over the inner side of each pita round. Cut each round into 8 wedges and place them in a single layer on ungreased cookie sheets.

3. Bake 10 minutes, or until golden and crisp.

Wonton Crisps

Most supermarkets sell three-inch-square wonton skins packaged in the freezer or specialty produce section, and you can find them fresh in the refrigerator sections of Asian markets. Sometimes the skins stick together, so be sure to separate them so they are one layer thick. These are easy to fry up until crunchy, and they can be seasoned sweetly or savory, depending upon the dip for which they are intended.

> Vegetable oil, for frying
> 50 wonton skins, 1 (12-ounce) package
> Kosher (coarse) salt
> Ground cumin, curry powder, cinnamon, or dried thyme leaves

1. Heat about 2 inches of oil in a deep-fat fryer, large deep skillet, or large saucepan to 340°F on a deep-fat thermometer.

2. While the oil is heating, cut each wonton skin diagonally in half to make 2 triangles from each square. In batches, lower the triangles, a few at a time, into the hot oil and cook, turning with tongs or a wire skimmer, for about 15 seconds a side, until golden and crisp. Remove with a slotted spoon and drain on paper towels.

3. While the wonton crisps are still warm, sprinkle them with salt to taste and dust lightly with the spice or herb of your choice. These will stay crisp for up to a week in a sealed plastic bag or an airtight container.

Crostini

Remember garlic toast? Well, crostini is simply the Italian name for it, though the authentic version implies a crisp, rather than the thick, doughy bread we used to shovel down with gobs of red sauce. I've made these extra thin, so you can use them as a base for a spread or as dippers.

Tip: To help slice the bread thinly, partially freeze it and use a sharp, heavy serrated knife. If the bread is not firm, you may have to slice it a little thicker, in which case the yield will be smaller.

    1 baguette (about 18 inches long), cut into ¼-inch-thick slices
    3 or 4 garlic cloves, cut in half
    3 tablespoons extra-virgin olive oil
    Kosher (coarse) salt

1. Preheat the oven to 400°F. Arrange the bread slices on large baking sheets in a single layer. Do them in batches if necessary. Toast the bread in the oven until golden brown and crisp, about 10 minutes.

2. Remove from the oven and rub the top of each slice with the cut side of a garlic clove. Then brush lightly with olive oil. Season with salt to taste.

Nutty Tortilla Chips

I *call these* tortillas locas, *or "crazy chips," because they're so irresistible you'll eat them like crazy. The same technique can also be used for tasty dippers made with split pita breads. For a spicier version of these same chips, substitute chili powder for the allspice.*

1/4 cup shelled pistachios or other nuts

2 tablespoons sesame seeds

1/2 teaspoon grated allspice or ground cinnamon

1/2 teaspoon salt

1 egg, lightly beaten

10 whole wheat tortillas, 8 inches in diameter

1. Preheat the oven to 375°F. Finely mince the pistachio nuts with the sesame seeds or pulse in a mini processor. Do not grind to a paste. Stir in the allspice and salt.

2. Brush one side of each tortilla lightly with some egg. Sprinkle about 1/2 tablespoon of the nut mixture over each tortilla. Cut each round into 8 wedges and place them in a single layer on 2 large baking sheets; or use 1 sheet and prepare them in batches.

3. Bake 10 minutes, or until lightly browned and crisp.

Index

A

Adzuki beans, in Asian
    sesame bean spread,
    48
Almonds, toasted, in
    romesco sauce, 74
Anchovy(-ies)
  Austrian cheese spread
    with caraway and, 85
  and garlic dip, creamy,
    36
  and tuna dip, 24
Apple brandy, in chicken
    liver pâté with thyme
    and calvados, 71

Artichoke and crab
    spread, hot, 76
Arugula dip, 27
Asian sesame bean
    spread, 48
Asian spiced eggplant
    spread, 56
Austrian cheese spread
    with caraway and
    anchovies, 85
Avocado
  in guacamole with
    cilantro and tomato,
    spicy, 55
  to open, 55

B

Baba ganoush, 32
Banana salsa, 19
Barbecue sauce,
    Caribbean jerk, 58
Basil
  sun-dried tomato and
    goat cheese spread
    with fresh, 84
  white bean dip with
    sun-dried tomatoes
    and, 51
Bean(s)
  dip
    black-eyed pea,

herbed, 49
hummus, 44
red, ranch rider, 45
refried black, with
    melted jack, 46
white, with sun-dried
    tomatoes and basil,
    51
spread
    Asian sesame, 48
    white, rosemary and,
        with toasted walnuts,
        50
    pinto, in Asian sesame
        bean spread, 48
Black bean dip with
    melted jack, refried,
    46
Black-eyed pea dip,
    herbed, 49
Black olive and dried
    tomato tapenade, 41
Blue cheese
    and Cheddar spread,
        sherried, 80
    in party Roquefort
        cheese cake, 82
Bombay curry dip, 28
Brandied mushroom pâté,
    72

Brandy, apple, in chicken
    liver pâté with thyme
    and calvados, 71

C

Cake, Roquefort cheese,
    party, 82
Calvados, chicken liver
    pâté with thyme and,
    71
Caraway, Austrian cheese
    spread with anchovies
    and, 85
Caribbean jerk barbecue
    sauce, 58
Caviar dip, 70
Cheddar (cheese)
    and blue cheese
        spread, sherried, 80
    in chile con queso, 86
Cheese
    cake, party Roquefort,
        82
    Jack, melted, refried
        black bean dip with,
        46
    spread
        with caraway and

anchovies, Austrian,
    85
Cheddar and blue,
    sherried, 80
goat, and sun-dried
    tomato, with fresh
    basil, 84
herbed garlic, 81
Chicken liver pâté with
    calvados and thyme, 71
Chickpeas, in hummus, 44
Chile con queso, 86
Chile (peppers)
    about, 46, 53–54
    chipotle
        about, 53
        -lime cream, 61
        mayonnaise, 29
    in guacamole with
        cilantro and tomato,
        spicy, 55
    jerk barbecue sauce,
        Caribbean, 58
    and plum tomato
        dipping sauce, Santa
        Fe, 64
    to tame heat, 54
    wasabi and mustard
        mayonnaise, East-
        West, 62

Chipotle (chiles)
about, 53
-lime cream, 61
mayonnaise, 29
Chips
herbed pita, 88
nutty tortilla, 91
Chutney ham spread, 30
Cilantro, spicy guacamole
with tomato and, 55
Clam digger's dip, 23
Corn
salsa with tomatillos,
peppers, and lime,
grilled, 12
white, in pineapple-
mango salsa, 14
Crab and artichoke
spread, hot, 76
Cranberry-orange salsa,
11
Cream, chipotle-lime, 61
Creamy garlic and
anchovy dip, 36
Crisps, wonton, 89
Crostini, 90
Cucumber and minted
yogurt dip, 40
Curry dip, Bombay, 28

D

Dijon mustard, in wasabi
and mustard mayon-
naise, East-West, 62
Dilled smoked salmon
spread, 68
Dippers
crostini, 90
herbed pita chips, 88
tortilla chips, nutty, 91
wonton crisps, 89
Dipping sauce
chile and plum tomato,
Santa Fe, 64
peanut, 60
Dip(s). *See also* Elegant
dips and spreads; Fast
and easy dips and
spreads; Spicy dips
and spreads
arugula, 27
baba ganoush, 32
bean
black-eyed pea, herbed,
49
hummus, 44
red, ranch rider, 45
refried black, with
melted jack, 46

white, with sun-dried
tomatoes and basil,
51
black olive and dried
tomato tapenade, 41
caviar, 70
chile con queso, 86
chipotle mayonnaise, 29
clam digger's, 23
cucumber and minted
yogurt, 40
curry, Bombay, 28
garlic
anchovy and, creamy,
36
baba ganoush, 32
cucumber and minted
yogurt, 40
mashed potato, with
garlic and walnuts,
Greek, 38
pesto, 27
red-hot orange spiced,
25
romesco sauce, 74
spinach, 26
tuna and anchovy, 24
watercress, 26
Dried tomato tapenade,
black olive and, 41

E

East-West wasabi and
    mustard mayonnaise,
    62
Easy dips and spreads. *See*
    Fast and easy dips
    and spreads
Eggplant(s)
    in baba ganoush, 32
    spread, Asian spiced, 56
Elegant dips and spreads
    brandied mushroom
        pâté, 72
    caviar dip, 70
    chicken liver pâté with
        calvados and thyme,
        71
    crab and artichoke
        spread, hot, 76
    dilled smoked salmon
        spread, 68
    green olive and walnut
        pesto, 77
    romesco sauce, 74
    smoked trout, potted, 69

F

Fast and easy dips and
    spreads
    Bombay curry dip, 28
    chipotle mayonnaise, 29
    chutney ham spread, 30
    clam digger's dip, 23
    red-hot orange spiced
        dip, 25
    tuna and anchovy dip, 24
    watercress dip, 26
Fresh tomato salsa, 9

G

Garbanzo beans (chick-
    peas), in hummus, 44
Garlic (garlicky)
    dip
        anchovy and, creamy, 36
        baba ganoush, 32
        cucumber and minted
        yogurt, 40
    freshness of, 31
    mashed potato dip with
        walnuts and, Greek, 38
    for mellower flavor, 28
    to peel cloves, 36

    roasted, in romesco
        sauce, 74
    spread
        cheese, herbed, 81
        roasted, 34
    tapenade, black olive and
        dried tomato, 41
Goat cheese
    in herbed garlic cheese
        spread, 81
    and sun-dried tomato
        spread with fresh
        basil, 84
Greek mashed potato
    dip with garlic and
    walnuts, 38
Green olive and walnut
    pesto, 77
Grilled corn salsa with
    tomatillos, peppers,
    and lime, 12
Guacamole with cilantro
    and tomato, spicy, 55

H

Ham spread, chutney, 30
Herbed black-eyed pea
    dip, 49

Herbed garlic cheese
spread, 81
Herbed pita chips, 88
Hot crab and artichoke
spread, 76
Hummus, 44

I

Ice bowl, 5

J

Jalapeño peppers, about,
53
Jerk barbecue sauce,
Caribbean, 58
Jicama-orange salsa, 20

K

Kalamata olives, in black
olive and dried
tomato tapenade, 41

L

Lime
-chipotle cream, 61
grilled corn salsa with
tomatillos, peppers,
and, 12

M

Mango
in chutney ham spread,
30
in jerk barbecue sauce,
Caribbean, 58
to peel, 15
-pineapple salsa, 14
Mashed potato dip with
garlic and walnuts,
Greek, 38
Mayonnaise
chipotle, 29
wasabi and mustard,
East-West, 62
Minted peach salsa with
toasted pecans, 16
Minted yogurt dip,
cucumber and, 40

Monterey Jack cheese,
melted, refried black
bean dip with, 46
Mushroom pâté, brandied,
72
Mustard and wasabi
mayonnaise, East-
West, 62

N

Nutty tortilla chips, 91

O

Olive
black, and dried tomato
tapenade, 41
green, and walnut pesto,
77
Onions, for milder flavor,
8
Orange
-cranberry salsa, 11
-jicama salsa, 20
spiced dip, red-hot, 25

P

Papaya, in jerk barbecue
    sauce, Caribbean, 58
Party Roquefort cheese
    cake, 82
Pâté
  brandied mushroom, 72
  chicken liver, with
      calvados and thyme,
      71
Peach salsa with toasted
    pecans, minted, 16
Peanut(s)
  dipping sauce, 60
  roasted, in watermelon
      salsa, 17
Pecans, minted peach
    salsa with toasted, 16
Peppers, grilled corn salsa
    with tomatillos, lime,
    and, 12
Pesto
  dip, 27
  green olive and walnut,
      77
Pineapple-mango salsa, 14
Pinto beans, in Asian
    sesame bean spread,
    48

Pita chips, herbed, 88
Plum tomato and chile
    dipping sauce, Santa
    Fe, 64
Potato dip with garlic and
    walnuts, Greek
    mashed, 38
Potted smoked trout, 69

Q

Quick dips and spreads.
    See Fast and easy dips
    and spreads

R

Ranch rider red bean dip,
    45
Red-hot orange spiced
    dip, 25
Red peppers, sweet
  roasted, in chipotle
      mayonnaise, 29
  in romesco sauce, 74
Refried black bean dip
    with melted jack, 46
Roasted garlic spread, 34

Roasted peanuts, in
    watermelon salsa, 17
Roasted vegetable salsa,
    18
Romesco sauce, 74
Roquefort cheese cake,
    party, 82
Rosemary and white bean
    spread with toasted
    walnuts, 50

S

Salmon, smoked, spread,
    dilled, 68
Salsa
  banana, 19
  chile con queso, 86
  cranberry-orange, 11
  grilled corn, with tomati-l
      los, peppers, and
      lime, 12
  minted peach, with
      toasted pecans, 16
  orange-jicama, 20
  pineapple-mango, 14
  roasted vegetable, 18
  tomato, fresh, 9
  verde, 10

watermelon, 17
Santa Fe chile and plum
     tomato dipping sauce,
     64
Sauce
  dipping
     chile and plum tomato,
        Santa Fe, 64
     peanut, 60
     jerk barbecue,Caribbean,
        58
     romesco, 74
Scotch bonnet pepper, in
     jerk barbecue sauce,
     Caribbean, 58
Sesame bean spread,
     Asian, 48
Sherried Cheddar and
     blue cheese spread,
     80
Skordelia (Greek mashed
     potato dip with garlic
     and walnuts), 38
Smoked salmon spread,
     dilled, 68
Smoked trout, potted, 69
Spicy dips and spreads
  chile and plum tomato
     dipping sauce, Santa
     Fe, 64

chipotle-lime cream, 61
eggplant spread, Asian
     spiced, 56
guacamole with cilantro
     and tomato, 55
jerk barbecue sauce,
     Caribbean, 58
peanut dipping sauce, 60
red-hot orange spiced
     dip, 25
wasabi and mustard
     mayonnaise, East-
     West, 62
Spinach dip, 26
Spread(s). See also
     Elegant dips and
     spreads; Fast and easy
     dips and spreads;
     Spicy dips and
     spreads
  black olive and dried
     tomato tapenade, 41
  brandied mushroom
     pâté, 72
  cheese. See Cheese
     spread(s)
  chicken liver pâté with
     calvados and thyme,
     71
  chipotle mayonnaise, 29

chutney ham, 30
crab and artichoke, hot,
     76
dilled smoked salmon, 68
garlicky. See Garlic
     (garlicky)
green olive and walnut
     pesto, 77
sesame bean, Asian, 48
smoked trout, potted, 69
Sun-dried tomato(es)
  and black olive tapenade,
     41
  and goat cheese spread
     with fresh basil, 84
  white bean dip with basil
     and, 51

T

Tahini, about, 33, 44
Tapenade, black olive and
     dried tomato, 41
Thyme, chicken liver pâté
     with calvados and, 71
Toasted almonds, in
     romesco sauce, 74
Toasted pecans, minted
     peach salsa with, 16

Toasted walnuts, rosemary
and white bean
spread with, 50
Tomatillos
grilled corn salsa with
peppers, lime, and, 12
in salsa verde, 10
Tomato(es)
plum, and chile dipping
sauce, Santa Fe, 64
salsa
in chile con queso, 86
fresh, 9
spicy guacamole with
cilantro and, 55
sun-dried
and black olive tape-
nade, 41
and goat cheese spread
with fresh basil, 84
white bean dip with
basil and, 51
Tortilla chips, nutty, 91
Trout, smoked, potted, 69
Tuna and anchovy dip, 24

Tzatziki (cucumber and
minted yogurt dip),
40

U

Umeboshi, in Asian
sesame bean spread,
48

V

Vegetable salsa, roasted,
18
Verde, salsa, 10

W

Walnut(s)
and green olive pesto, 77
mashed potato dip with
garlic and, Greek, 38

toasted, rosemary and
white bean spread
with, 50
Wasabi and mustard
mayonnaise, East-
West, 62
Watercress dip, 26
Watermelon salsa, 17
White bean
dip with sun-dried toma-
toes and basil, 51
and rosemary spread
with toasted walnuts,
50
Wonton crisps, 89

Y

Yogurt
cheese, 81
in herbed garlic cheese
spread, 81
dip, cucumber and
minted, 40